Wings of the Black Cross

PHOTO ALBUM OF LUFTWAFFE AIRCRAFT

by Jerry Crandall

Illustrated by Thomas A. Tullis

NUMBER ONE

Eagle Editions Ltd.

The first of six photos, appearing on the following pages, of an interesting Fw 190 A-2, W. Nr. 513. The tactical number appears to be "Red 17". The Yellow spinner, under cowl and rudder, plus the heavily mottled with what seems to be Dark Green, all contribute to make this a very colorful machine. The area in Germany is unknown.

The inboard 20 mm cannons are still in place but the outboard guns have been removed.

"Red 17" Fw 190 A-2. The H2 early *Hakenkreuz*, Yellow rudder and early style upper wing cross are still intact, but the port side fuselage cross has been burned away.

An American G.I. standing next to the tail of W. Nr. 513. The H2 early style *Hakenkreuz*, Black with White border and thin Black outline, is very clear. The heavy mottling has partially obscured the *Werknummer*.

Notice the yellow rudder appears lighter in this photo than in the previous images. The standard canopy with the late-style armored head rest and solid main wheels have been retrofitted. The early B2 style fuselage *Balkenkreuz* can barely be seen.

Now this aircraft has been moved to a hanger. The late solid wheels and under wing cross is in good view. Note the Yellow rudder, spinner and under cowl also appear lighter in value in this image, due to a different film type from the first four photos.

An Fw 190 A-7 W. Nr. 34028? with part of a light colored "4" remaining on the damaged fuselage. the blown canopy is probably a retrofit as it is unusual for an A-7 to be so equipped. The fuselage cross is the simple Black outline B4 style. Area and date not known, photo is signed "Love Pete".

Fw 190 F-9 W. Nr. 426050 at Schleißheim, Germany Fall 1945. No tactical number. The tail wheel yoke is configured for carrying torpedoes. Late war combination of Dark Gray over a Light color base coat is evident on wings and horizontal tail.

Fw 190 "Yellow 4". Note open radio access panel that appears to be reinforced wood. Darmstadt, Germany. May 1945.

Fw 190 A-8 coded DU + JP, W. Nr. 17001(6?). Upper surface incorporating late war combination of Dark Gray over a Light color base coat is especially notable on upper wings. In foreground is Bf 109 G-10 "Black 11" W. Nr. 770194. Photo taken at Prien, southern Germany.

Fw 190 A-6 "White 2" W. Nr. 550503. Built by the Ago Factory at Oschersleben, Germany. This aircraft was formerly with II. / SG 2 photo taken at Kitzingen, Germany. The B4 style *Balkenkreuz* is somewhat unusual to see on an Fw 190 A-6.

Fw 190 "White 10" possibly a machine used by a *Schlachtgeschwader* unit. Desert camouflage with RLM 79 *Sandgelb* and RLM 80 Dark Green spots.

Wels, Austria airfield filled with machines that fled the Eastern Front, mostly aircraft from *Luftflotte* 4 having the prescribed Yellow rudders and cowl bands. Note the Ju 87 D in the foreground, various Bf 109 and Fw 190 aircraft in the right background and a Ju 52 in the center. More Fw 190 F-8s can be seen in the left foreground including "Yellow 8" of a II. *Gruppe Schlachtgeshwader* unit. May 1945.

Another view of the Wels, Austria airfield. A Ju 52, Ju 87 Stuka, Fw 190 F-8 and two Bf 109 Gs can be identified. Note the Yellow fuselage bands and the overall dark camouflage on the Bf 109s.

Fw 190 F-8 Fighter bombers from a II. *Gruppe Schlacht-geschwader* unit from *Luftflotte* 4. The Fw 190 A-8 on the far left has an overall dark camouflage color.
Wels, Austria May 1945.

A strange hybrid Fw 190 with a short cowling like an Fw 190 A-2 or A-3 but the *werknummer* ?35435 indicates a late sub-type. Other features indicative of a late sub-type are the solid wheels, 3.3 meter VDM 9-12153A metal propeller with the external bolt-on pitch weights, and the late war style markings. Note the small White square containing the letter "A" on the rear fuselage, also the dark lower portion of the landing gear door. Sitting in the cockpit is William Goldsmith, a member of the 6th Armored Division. This Fw 190 was found at the large training school at Altenburg, Eastern Germany.

William Goldsmith, an armor salvage specialist, standing next to a burned-out Fw 190 F-8, W. Nr. 581679 found among many machines at the training at Altenburg, Germany. Note the Ju 87 in the background.

An Fw 190 F-8 "Black 5" from a III. *Gruppe* of *Luftflotte* 4 with the Yellow cowl band and rudder. Faintly visible is an over-painted *Stab* chevron and bar under the "5". Frankfurt am Main, Germany 30 April 1945.

Fw 190 S two-seat trainer coded BU + DY "Yellow 29" on rear fuselage.

First of four images of an Fw 190 F-9 with simplified late-war camouflage. The under wing is natural metal with Red-Oxide ailerons, B4 style Black out line cross and large wooden paddle bladed propeller. Still attached to the aircraft is the late-war E2 light steel drop tank.

A slightly different view of the same Fw 190 F-9, American G.I. poses right in front of the abandoned aircraft.

The large wooden propeller and heavy armored cowl ring are featured in this view of this Fw 190 F-9, parked in a heavily wooded revetment.

Now this Fw 190 F-9 has been moved out of the revetment to a large hangar. Note the drop tank is still attached. April 1945.

Light Green dappled spots of camouflage are on this Bf 109 G-6 W. Nr. 410061 built by the Erla factory found at Wunsdorf, Germany. A similar photo can be found on the cover of the excellent Broken Eagles 3 by Carl Hildebrandt. Other Bf 109s with this camouflage were found at Pilsen, Czechoslovakia.

William Goldsmith of the 6th Armored Division leaning on a Bf 109 G-14 "Black 7". Altenburg, Germany, May 1945. Note Burned out Fw 190 in background.

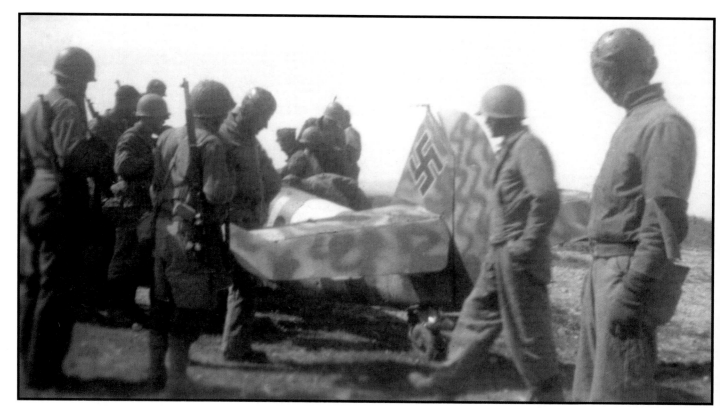

American Armor and Infantry personnel examine a downed Bf 109 G-2. The colorful camouflage is RLM 79 *Sandgelb* with wavey lines of RLM 80 Dark Green. The White theater band can be seen but the tactical number is not visible.

Front view of the previous Bf 109 G-2. The White spinner and over-painted JG 53 emblem on the engine cowl are of interest. Somewhere in North Africa. Date unknown.

An interesting and puzzling Bf 109 G-6 "White I" W. Nr. 160087 of JG 53. Note the Yellow undercowling, White and RLM 70 Black-Green sectioned spinner. Found at Braunschardt, Germany.

This photo reveals the letter "I", the meaning of which is not known. The Red fuselage band was possibly carried over from 1943 as most machines carried the designated Black home defense bands after August 1944. Of special interest is the Bf 110 style radio antenna barely visible under the rear fuselage. This aircraft may have been used for radio experimentation or training purposes.

An American Lieutenant leaning on Bf 109 K-4 "Yellow 13" of 15./JG 53 (IV. *Gruppe*). This K-4 camouflage pattern identifies it as being in the 332XXX range. The colors are RLM 76 under surfaces, RLM 75 Gray-Violet and RLM 83 Dark Green upper surfaces. Part of the Black RV home defense band and the tip of the Yellow *Welle* (Wave) can be seen on the right. Note the fuel octane triangle has been cut out for a souvenir. Koblenz, Germany 10 March 1945.

A Group of 32 Bf 109 K-4 fuselages found at the Messerschmitt factory at Regensburg, Germany. The distinctive camouflage patterns of the 332XXX range are clearly evident in this photo. See Japo's book *Messerschmitt Bf 109 K Camouflage and Markings* Page 42 for other photos of Regensburg Bf 109 K machines.

A captured Bf 109 G-4/R6 of 364 *Squadrilla*, 150° *Gruppo* of the *Regia Aeronautica*. The aircraft is undergoing disassembly by the Americans and the 20 mm under wing gondolas have been removed.

Note the Yellow under cowling, White nose band and fuselage band, the normal White tail cross appears to be mostly obliterated. Sicily, 1943.

Bf 109 K-4 "White 6" of 9./JG 27 (III. *Gruppe*) apparently in the 330XXX *Werknummer* range. May 1945, area in Germany not known.

Two unidentified aircrew pose with a Bf 109 G fuselage "Black 2" trimmed in Red found at Achmer airfield near Osnabrück, Germany by the Dutch 320 Squadron of the RAF. Note their B-25s in the background. The C3 octane triangle is visible on the Bf 109 G fuselage.

Bf 109 G-14/AS W. Nr. 784930 "Red 1" of I./JG 77 with the White and Green home defense band.
This aircraft had been flying *Jabo* missions, see the tail fin portion of the SD 250 bomb on the ground.

Bf 109 K-4 W. Nr. 332579 "Black 15" of IV./JG 53 found at Schleißheim, Germany, fall 1945. Camouflage
is typical of the 332XXX *werknummer* range of RLM 76 under surfaces and upper surface segments of
RLM 75 Gray-Violet and RLM 83 Dark Green. The Black JG 53 home defense band with the Black
trimmed in White *Welle* (Wave) and spiral spinner are also noteworthy. The next aircraft is a Bf 109 F-
4 W. Nr. 7551 (stenciled on the fuselage) coded TS + MB with a G-type engine cowling.

Do 335 A-1 W. Nr. 24016?. Captured by American forces and given to the British, but crash landed at Merville, France in December 1945 in transit, and never made it to England.

Another view of Do 335 A-1 W. Nr. 24016?. The American star and bar have been painted out before turning the aircraft over to the British. Photos taken at Neubiberg, Germany.

Do 335 A-1 W. Nr. 240161 found at Oberpfaffenhofen, Germany and shipped to U.S. as FE 1012. The #1 on the tail is the last digit of the *Werknummer* and the 3 represents model number 3.

Bf 110 G-2 of Hans Kogler *Gruppenkommandeur* of II./ZG 26. This aircraft may also have been flown at times by Wilhelm Teske, Kogler's wingman. Note the single command chevron and White fuselage band.

Side view of the same aircraft. In the foreground, broken loose as a result of the crash landing is the M 1 cannon pod that houses the twin 20 mm cannons.

Ju 87 G-2 W. Nr. 494200, no codes are visible. Captured at Pilsen, Czechoslovakia, May 1945. The Yellow rudder and cowl band identifies it as being from *Luftflotte* 4.

A frontal view of the same Ju 87 G-2 with 37 mm cannons mounted under the wings.

Ju 188 A found at Innsbruck, Austria, May 1945. Note radar antenna on the starboard wing.

Close up of the cockpit area, note the mount for the forward-firing MG 151 20 mm cannon.

American soldiers looking over a Bf 110 G-4 night fighter in excellent condition. Note the attractive spiral spinners and the 300 liter drop tanks are still attached. Also note the flame dampeners are mounted on the engine exhaust. Regretfully the codes are not known.

Not much left of this Ju 88 G-1 night fighter with FuG 220 S-2 radar. It does show off some interesting camouflage on the upper wing and engine nacelles. One is overall dark with light spots while the other nacelle is partially dark with the center section overall light. Both spinners are a very light color. The cross hatching effect on the port spinner is caused by camouflage netting.

Ta 154 A-1 W. Nr. 320003 sitting in a wooded revetment. The camouflage is typical of late war Luftwaffe night fighters, overall RLM 76 Light Blue with RLM 75 Gray-Violet spots, on the upper fuselage and vertical tail.

Same Ta 154 as above, looking out into the meadow that was used as the airfield. The upper horizontal tail and wings have a splinter pattern with Dark Gray segments

Two American G.I.s in front of an Arado 96 coded K? + VE with a Yellow fuselage
band a number '?4" on the fin. Behind is a Bf 109 G-6 or G-14 "Black 51".

Two different American soldiers in front of the Arado 96 and Bf 109
as pictured above, at München-Riem, Germany, 4 June 1945.

Arado 96 W. Nr. 550784 coded VH + LH. Interesting features include wide Yellow band behind the rear 'H', and on stenciled on the vertical fin the location of the A/B 72 school at Lake Schwerin in Eastern Germany which also includes the telephone number, Schwerin 2222.

A portion of Lake Schwerin can be seen behind the Arado 96
in this image of the same aircraft as pictured above.

Me 262 W. Nr. 110956 "White 17" of III./EJG 2. This machine is camouflaged in the early Me 262 scheme of RLM 76 under surfaces, RLM 75/RLM 74 upper surfaces. The front portion of the port engine cowling is unpainted. A published color photo exists of this aircraft.

Me 262 W. Nr. 113345 being examined by American G.I.s.

Among the Fw 190s and a Ju 88 night fighter at the München, Germany
airfield scrap heap is an unpainted Me 262 W. Nr. 111728. May 1945.

A close-up of W. Nr. 111728. The gray putty used to fill the panel line seams
is evident and the last three digits of the W. Nr. '728' are on the bomb rack.

One of the many Me 262s found in the woods next to the München *autobahn*.
This unpainted one has no engines and no markings of any kind.

Me 262 C-2b W. Nr. 170074. This aircraft was used to test BMW 003 engines. In the background is me 262 V 10 W. Nr. 130005 used in towing and bomb-dropping feasibility tests. Lechfeld, Germany.

Remains of an Me 262 sitting on a log ramp just off the *autobahn* in south Germany. 27 April 1945.

American soldiers dis-assembling an Me 262 found in the woods
near München, Germany, possibly a former JV 44 aircraft. May 1945.

Mistel S 2 Fw 190 F-8 and Ju 88 G-1 W. Nr. 714790 combination, discovered at Ludwigslust, Germany, May 1945. Both aircraft have Red tipped spinners. The Fw 190 has a small number '90' on the rudder. See Classic Publications' book *Mistels* by Robert Forsyth for more photos and details.

Mistel S-2 Fw 190 A-8 and Ju 88 G-1 W. Nr. 714237 combination found at Merseburg, Germany, May 1945. Note Red star centered in fuselage *Balkenkreuz* on Ju 88 which is a former night fighter from NJG 5.

Another view of the 2 Mistel combinations found at the Junkers facility at Merseburg, Germany, May 1945.

"Red 17" Fw 190 A-2 W. Nr. 513. See pages 2, 3 and 4 for photos.
Colors: Undersurfaces RLM 65 or RLM 76 Light Blue, Uppersurfaces base coat RLM 02/RLM 71. Heavily mottled with Dark Green. RLM 04 Yellow spinner, undercowl and rudder. Note fuselage *Balkenkreuz* has been scorched off.

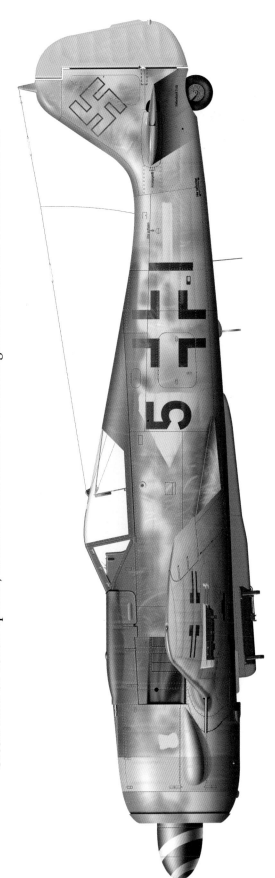

"Black 5" Fw 190 F-8 from a III. *Gruppe* of *Luftflotte* 4. Frankfurt am Main, Germany, 30 April 1945. See page 10 for photo.
Colors: Undersurfaces RLM 76, Uppersurfaces RLM 75/74. Black exhaust area, RLM 04 Yellow stripe on cowling and rudder per *Luftflotte* 4 directive. Note previous *Stab* markings slightly visible.

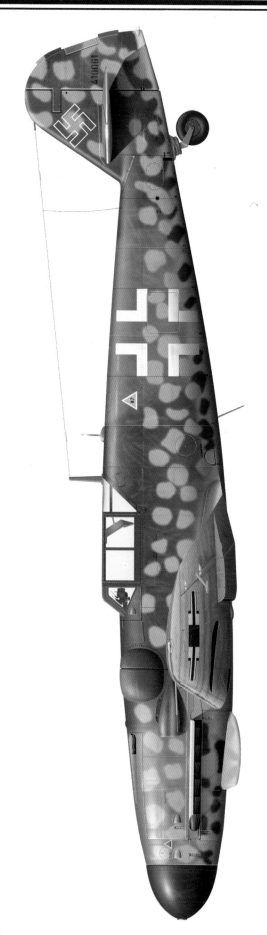

Bf 109 G-6 W. Nr. 410061, Wunsdorf, Germany, May 1945. See page 13 for photo.
Colors: Undersurfaces RLM 76 Light Blue, Uppersurfaces RLM 75/74. Fuselage heavily dappled with Light Green spots.

"White I" Bf 109 G-6 W. Nr. 160087 JG 53. Braunschardt, Germany. See page 15 for photo.
Colors: Undersurfaces RLM 76 Light Blue, Uppersurfaces RLM 75/74. RLM 04 Yellow under cowling. RLM 23 Red home defense band. Spinner White and RLM 70 sectioned.

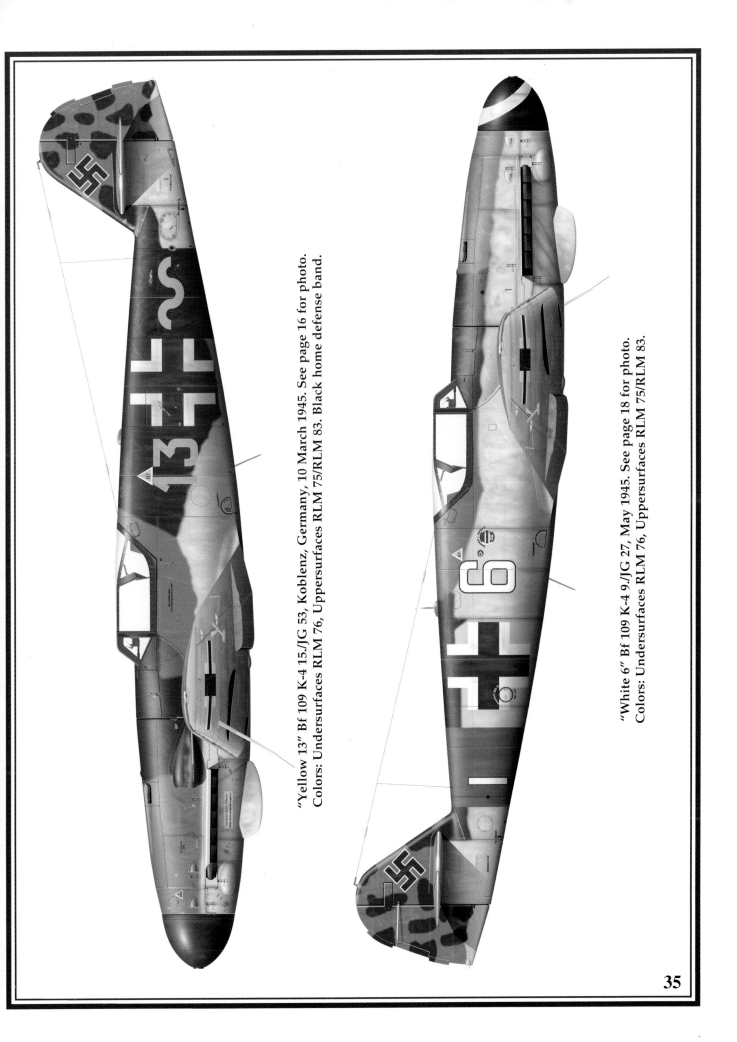

"Yellow 13" Bf 109 K-4 15./JG 53, Koblenz, Germany, 10 March 1945. See page 16 for photo. Colors: Undersurfaces RLM 76, Uppersurfaces RLM 75/RLM 83. Black home defense band.

"White 6" Bf 109 K-4 9./JG 27, May 1945. See page 18 for photo. Colors: Undersurfaces RLM 76, Uppersurfaces RLM 75/RLM 83.

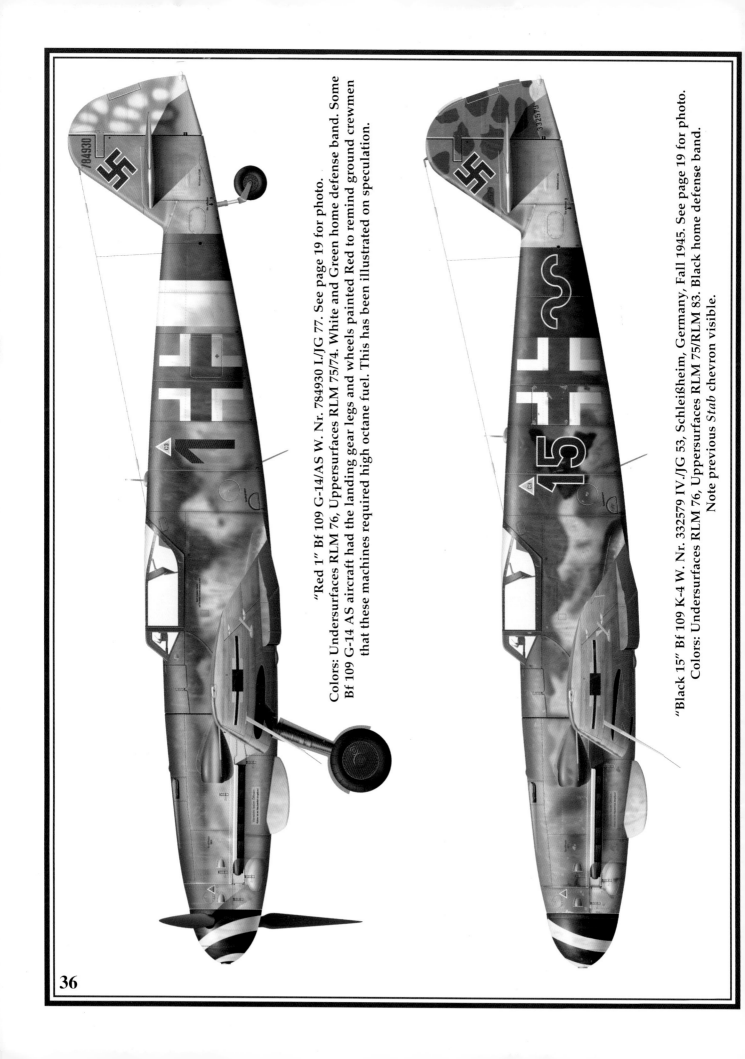

"Red 1" Bf 109 G-14/AS W. Nr. 784930 I./JG 77. See page 19 for photo.
Colors: Undersurfaces RLM 76, Uppersurfaces RLM 75/74. White and Green home defense band. Some Bf 109 G-14 AS aircraft had the landing gear legs and wheels painted Red to remind ground crewmen that these machines required high octane fuel. This has been illustrated on speculation.

"Black 15" Bf 109 K-4 W. Nr. 332579 IV./JG 53, Schleißheim, Germany, Fall 1945. See page 19 for photo.
Colors: Undersurfaces RLM 76, Uppersurfaces RLM 75/RLM 83. Black home defense band.
Note previous Stab chevron visible.